Merciful Days

MERCER UNIVERSITY PRESS

Endowed by

TOM WATSON BROWN
and
THE WATSON-BROWN FOUNDATION, INC.

Merciful Days

Poems

JESSE GRAVES

MERCER UNIVERSITY PRESS
Macon, Georgia
MMXX

MUP/ P611

Published by Mercer University Press
1501 Mercer University Drive
Macon, Georgia 31207

25 24 23 22 21 20   5 4 3 2 1

Books published by Mercer University Press are printed on acid-free paper
that meets the requirements of the American National Standard for
Information Sciences—Permanence of Paper for Printed Library Materials.

Printed and bound in the United States.

This book is set in Adobe Caslon Pro.

Cover/jacket design by Burt&Burt.

Library of Congress Cataloging-in-Publication Data
Names: Graves, Jesse, 1973- author.
Title: Merciful days : poems / Jesse Graves.
Description: Macon, Georgia : Mercer University Press, 2020. |
Identifiers: LCCN 2020027591 | ISBN 9780881467567 (paperback)
Subjects: LCGFT: Poetry.
Classification: LCC PS3607.R38625 M47 2020 | DDC 811/.6--dc23
LC record available at https://lccn.loc.gov/2020027591

This book is for my mother,
Joyce Ann Houston Graves—Joy to all who know her,
Who has always given me the words I needed

CONTENTS

I

II

Merciful Days

I

The Kingdom of the Dead

I have no crew nor fleet ship to carry me,
no ewe nor sleek ram to offer for bloodfeast,
but I seek no counsel with kings or warriors,

only the humble dead, those well-known to me
and few others, who reach out in dreams,
who call back from wherever they dwell.

I would guide my uncle out of the shadows
to tell again of his bucolic boyhood,
running through fields of burley tobacco leaves.

My brother hangs back, still new to his ghost-life.
How to bring him forward? Will he speak to me
about parting the veil between our worlds?

Not one shade who greets Odysseus and drinks
from the blood of his flocks bears welcome news.
Their lesson is slow suffering, awaiting hidden signs.

As in life, so in the burdened House of Death,
even those who walked in glory suffer here.
I fear what I will see, yet still long to see.

The Edges of Cornfields at Dusk

Driving east to west past midnight across
central Pennsylvania, I spot a crumpled
deer every five miles for a long grisly stretch.
After the fourth, I shake my head and blink
fast to clear the images, but my headlights
flare them and seem to make the splayed legs
flinch like they might jump up and run
back into the forests recently departed.
I imagine bedding where the deer slept,
the edges of cornfields where they found
stalks to forage through dusk and early dark,
the soft sounds of their muzzles lapping
creeks in the back corners of Berks County.
Something in the reflection of glazed eyes
beckons me toward the rut of road shoulder.
In my waking dream, I lift them off the pavement
and back into the weathered grass by the interstate,
some words trying to form in my tight throat
about the fields they will graze in their next bodies.

Distant Star

The old red truck was always getting stuck in a ditch,
or the David Brown tractor bogged deep in mud.
My father would wave his arms and shout instructions
on what lever to pull, which post to hitch to the chain,
the place to lean my shoulder against and shove.
Sometimes I reminded him where he was, in bed,
in the old blue room, in the house he has owned
almost fifty years, longer than my whole life.
But other times, when his eyes fixed on some
distant star in the far corner of the ceiling,
I tried my hardest to dig, to drag, to gouge,
anything to loosen the grip of the muck
that pulls him out of the world he has known.
The skin that hangs so loosely on his bones
tells me how few of these strained days are left,
the thin rasp of his breath drifting into the room
means goodbye, that word I am not ready to hear.

Challenger

For My Mother, Turning 76

Remember when we fed the cows
from the window of the barn loft?
We had the jumpy black Angus then,
years before the docile polled Herefords
who mill meekly about, globe-eyed.

Today the sun is out, and we celebrate
in short sleeves in early November,
and watch for leaves to drop from
red-orange maples, but that morning
blowing snow kept me home from school.

We fed the square bales then, misshapen
as they were, and I loved to cut the twine
with the short blade of my pocket knife,
taut forms loosening and scattering
apart on the way to the ground below.

Our mistake was to call the cows too soon,
"S'Cavs, S'Cavs," just as my father said it,
my father who was on the road in hard
weather, probably a 36-hour run to Harrisburg,
driving through ice to get home by midnight.

In half a second, it seemed, the whole herd
circled beneath us, grunting and jostling,
and you said, "Shit fire!" which made me laugh
so hard I lost my breath, and could not even
throw the hay out of the loft to distract them.

We escaped, of course, and like so many other
mornings after our chores, you said, "I think
we need some biscuits, don't you?"
"With apple butter," I said, and you held
my collar as I climbed down the slick ladder.

While cups of hot chocolate warmed our fingers,
we turned to the one tv channel we could
watch without static, and saw a real rocket ship,
like the model I wanted for Christmas, explode right
on screen, again and again, in spiraling slow motion.

I looked at you, as I always did when I could not
understand what I saw, and your mouth frozen
in mid-gasp silently told me, on the coldest day
of the year, that in a particle of that churning smoke
departed the childhood I thought would last forever.

Nameless River

I am trying to find a name this afternoon,
wandering through the lately abandoned
storehouse of my father's memories.

He left my life with the key still in his pocket,
so I enter through the high cracked window
of his stories, looking for what to call the man

who offered him that first job driving a truck,
training him for three days, then sending
him for an overnight run to Lexington.

Clyde Ivey sounds true to my ear, slow note
of the long *I* gliding through the name,
his whole life eliding in the sudden moment

when his tow-rig hit a patch of night-time ice.
Clyde had gone to pick up some poor country boy
who cb-radioed for help, stranded on a twisting

mountain road whose curves are buried away now,
like Clyde Ivey, who spun through the guardrail
into the nameless river pushing hard below.

Sage Grass Brushing Against My Shins

I went to bed thinking about how my father
died, trying to exhaust myself silently repeating
his question, "How can you let them do this to me?"
Sometime in the night, I fell into a dream
where he was old and sick, but alive, and the family
had gathered around him for Thanksgiving.
After the meal, we went outside and wandered
around the yard, scattering cornbread to chickens,
scratching the heads of all the dogs we've ever had.
I followed my dad past the barn to the pond
we dug together, listening as he told me how to clear
the pine saplings thickening along the banks.
The dream carried me along like real life,
and I could feel the sage grass brushing against
my shins as we walked back through the field.
The kids had all lined up to play football,
which we haven't done since I was a child,
before my brother died, before my uncle died.
My daughter Chloe, a girl again, picked the teams,
"I want Pap on my side," she shouted, making my dad
grin and blush, and say, "No, no, I'm too old."
"That doesn't matter," my daughter said, and I loved
her more right then even than the dream itself,
more than I hated how soon I would wake.

Merciful Days

My mother and I walk the cattle trail
alongside the family cemetery fence.
Mid-February feels like late May
with grass in the fields turning green.
At a distance, a faint red tint appears
along the branches of bare trees,
like a chemical mist settling among them,
false dawn promising new leaves.
"Just you watch," she says, "everything
will bloom out, thinking springtime
is here, and then we'll get a freeze."
We make another round, circling
the ones we love and have lost,
separated by the breath we breathe
and the dirt that covers them.
She sighs, almost a word emerging
through the air she pushes out, almost
saying she is tired of it, the way it keeps
moving through her. "Merciful days,"
she says, meaning something I feel,
but cannot begin to shape into words.

Old Man Wandering the Roads

My grandfather grafted trees and sold the shoots
across four counties to farmers who wanted
new fruit for canning, an apricot or yellow pear,
jar of late autumn to sweeten winter bread.

He left a trail of growing things wherever he went,
and carried a little change in his pockets
to prove he had done his day of work,
maybe not a lot of it, but enough to get around,

enough to buy gas for an old Ford, Coca-Cola
for the road, sardines and saltines for dinner.
I remember him as a talker who visited often
but never stayed long, sitting shoulders forward

on our couch, cradling an empty coffee cup,
anxious to tell where he'd been that morning
as my father listened with his eyes cast down,
trying not to notice split seams and unlaced shoes.

"Old man wandering the roads," my mother said,
clearing plates and cups once he was gone.
And each time my father went outside with him
when he left, walked him slowly to his truck,

but never came straight back into the house,
finding something always to do in the fields,
new ground ever to break, a stump to haul away,
some old animal dying and needing buried.

Come Running

They amble across the field, drawn to shade,
sniffing for uncropped clover and sprout,
their slowness measurable by galactic tilt.
From a distance the calves look identical,
but watch closely, and the shadings around
white faces range from salmon to maroon,
and the little curls on their foreheads
twist in tighter and looser tangles.
If a baby separates from its mother,
she calls for it like a foghorn, the lowing
anyone can tell means "find me now."
But listen closer, and a mother can signal
her child with the slightest grunt
from the other side of the field—
no other calf will move or even look up,
yet one comes running, summoned home.

Raft

Life there seemed never to change,
except around the edges of the yard
where leaves sprouted, turned colors,
fell carelessly away and started over again.

Then my grandfather died, who drove
his shaky truck around selling orchard trees.
Then my uncle Cotton died, who taught
me lonely old songs on his homemade guitar.

I watched my parents carry the sodden
weight of their sadness for a time,
finally returning to their regular lives,
without a father, without a favorite uncle.

And then I was different, sitting alone
on the raft of being twelve years old,
wanting something but not knowing what,
floating away from the unchanging life.

Tiny metal cars left in boxes, plastic soldiers
untouched for weeks, then for months,
childhood becoming a song I had forgotten
the words to— a tune I could no longer carry.

Katie Myers

We called the ridge after her, lonesome jagged
furrow that it peaked, barely level enough
ground to scratch out a road. *The cady mar*
was how it sounded in the olden tongue,

spoken still by ones too young to recall
who she was, or what she did, or how
she came to be there, alone, we heard,
in such as that dire, dreadful, sovereign place.

Never arable land, too steep for food crops,
for grazing animals, but neither was it barren.
Every bright kind of mountain wildflower
grew there, wild phlox, columbine, mayapple,

those good only for show, and those good
for bile, canker, thrush-mouth, and swimmy-head,
bitter roots boiled down to tea, or stirred round
with whiskey, rock candy, and glycerin.

She was none of the Fate Myers people,
or unclaimed kin if she was, those few who
prospered and lived in town, who bought up
all the roadside farms of the county seat.

Driving her ridge at night was riding with
the ghost, doing whatever she told you.
Her cabin stitched right into the forest floor,
windows without glass, door hanging

by the bottom hinge, like some drunkard flung
aside with one foot still planted firm.
The shingles seemed to reach across the road
toward the trees that were their ancestors.

She could have lived there, century before last,
if stories be trusted, if damp wood holds
together in that sunless stretch of slant,
where black snakes drape from the shoulder

so languorously car wheels catch and grind
them into strips like pink and black taffeta.
Once my grandfather told of a candle
wavering its lone flame in her window,

light where both sun and moon are strangers,
his car first slowing down, then taking off
full speed, exactly like his heartbeat,
her shadow, he hoped, left far behind.

Holocene

The boy raised in a valley keeps his eyes
on the skies as jet trails and chicken hawks
appear in their brief patterns and are gone.

He climbs ridges to see over the tree-line.
Distances ripple in shades of fainting blue
like hills breaking into mountainous waves.

The blush of color in leaves embarrasses him,
shapes of the trees' bodies now visible,
strange longings jostle him, make him look away.

Fields race through the seasons, tinted by each
bleaching hour, he has climbed so high,
he wants to see the world unfolding,

movement too slow to measure.
Earth crests along the deep skyline,
the amplitude of time thunders past.

Mossy Springs

Water surges out as cold as bright stars
look at night, aching your hands
as you cup a clean drink to your lips.

Standing under towering sycamores,
and shadow of the steep cliff that
gives the spring its source,

you wonder at the bloodlines
that drank here before you,
dating as far back as time records.

Hunters from the original tribes,
trackers chasing game upstream,
farmers drawn over from the fields,

and now you, looking for the lost
kingdom of your ancestors, dousing
their eternal thirst to be found.

History

Every hour changes something forever.
Or changes something for another hour.
Watch the clouds at the far end of sky,
how slowly they move toward you,
how the blue above seems inviolable.
Watch for a moment, and the mottled
streak of gray-threaded horizon
reaches over like a lid closing a box.
The box you live in feels like history,
permanent change and no warning,
myths of cycles and repetition.
The loop you cycle through is imaginary:
it's a new world every hour.
No history here.
Mountains for eternity, a few scattered
tribes, hunting and gathering,
supplanted by farmers, also hunting,
gathering, and going hungry most days,
then a railroad, a teachers' college,
highways, and chain restaurants.
When it all disappears, deer and coyotes
will stake out new feeding grounds,
trout will flourish in cold, swift streams,
mountains for eternity, clouds ever passing.

Barn Swallows

They made a sound like wind
coming to life, ignition that always
startled me, though I knew
the swallows would be sleeping there.
They hid where I wanted to hide,
high in the rafters, above the loft,
beyond the broken tobacco sticks,
unstrung bales of hay, cracked tires,
barbed edges of nails, staples, and wire.

The barn gave both work and shelter
from work, and late in the fall,
when leaves began to gather up
their transient colors and scatter
in hidden corners to crumble,
cracks in the barn walls whistled
and chimed, made soft music,
like rows of flutes and violins
played by an ensemble of ghosts.

I came there to make up child-games
among the throwaway parts,
build obstacle courses for bright
metal cars to race through.
I came there to disappear,
become a vessel for any message
the birds wanted to deliver,
wings fluttering along my spine,
voices like tiny bells in my ears.

At the Window

We always kept the birdfeeders full
at the house by Sapsucker Woods.
Even when the deer would come
during the night and stand on two legs
to eat the seeds and suet blocks.
I usually had the baby on my shoulder,
pointing out the different birds
that came skittering in for landing,
quick mouthful, then off again.
We walked like that from the window
to all the picture-frames on the walls
so she could reach out and tap
everyone on the nose, and I'd say "Bing!"
Then she would laugh, and we would
go heat a bowl of cereal, and slice
bananas—I could do everything with
one hand, it seemed—and sometimes we ate
sitting together on the floor.
We might have moved some plastic animals
in circles, or looked at pictures in a book
about rabbits or constellations,
then gone back to the window to see
whether any birds had come for brunch,
or if a squirrel had climbed the feeder-pole.
That was my life those days, one arm forever
full and wriggling, the other arm free
to do anything that needed doing,
like shushing away vagrant squirrels,
or waving off the future just a bit longer.

Lisa in the Forest

By creekside she learned mosses and ferns,
which ones grew tall and thin, feathery
as frayed linens, and which kept dense
like moist fur and thrived close to ground.

Now, she loves to find the maidenhair,
whose fronds reach up like the fingers
of her childhood hand waving
from the middle distance of times past.

We have walked a thousand miles
on trails and off, with me a step behind
so she can keep a clear view of fringed phacelia,
mayapple, Dutchmen's breeches, trillium.

Every flash of new color announces itself
to her eye, greener green, dirtier brown,
full spectrum fanning out like a wild library,
each sprig a volume in the catalogue of life.

Jewel

Morning emerges pink as a watermelon rind,
like the night has sucked some essential blood
from it, morning of delicate constitution,

singe of early light against rising blue mist.
Elsewhere there is destruction upon the land,
hatchet work of mass energy production,

elsewhere woodland cathedrals are stripped
of their white oak spires, wracked
by the terrible churning jaws of industry.

But not here, not yet, in this one side-pocket
of history, the channel through which money
sluiced toward the hardly touched West

where the American future awaited,
the emerald that is one sun-streaked corner
of Cumberland Mountain remains untouched.

Wind Work

Not all roads lead to the lake
in Sharps Chapel, but if you chase
switchbacks and keep heading west,
you will end up on the shale-ridge
that once traced the curves
of the river,
                    curves of the old river
drowned for decades under water,
land where my ancestors plotted
their lives invisible now to visitors
as jet trails after an hour of wind-work.

An hour of wind-work will stir
still surfaces into a swelling line,
into a pattern that moves toward shore ·
like smoke rising skyward,
                    and like smoke rising
I am drawn in a direction, back to this
water, the land underneath, where
my great-great-grandmother was buried,
and later unburied, dug out of the ground
like a root, replanted in strange soil,
spirit arrived, body never home again.

October Woods

The first cold nights have curled
the edges of forest floor ginger,
rouged the sumac and sugar maples,
cracked the caps of fallen acorns.
Mushrooms and polyps of lichen
thrive now, all shapes and colors
sprout from the loamy dirt.
Turkey-tail fungus fans across
the torsos of downed trees,
morning frost scintillating it all.

Hawks

Children of the hundred-year house,
house under the canopy, the overhang,
built before the chestnut blight,
Great Wars, Great Depression,
New Deal, and Trickle Down economics.
Nothing ever trickled down to us
except rain running off the tin roof.
Worms with black and yellow stripes
suctioned the catalpa leaves clean,
and at their fattest, I shot them
with my pump action BB gun.
I chased everything that moved,
but did not want to kill most of them.
I lived beneath a ridge named after
an old woman, Katie Myers,
so ancient only my grandmother
heard stories about her.
Hawks skirred the ridgeline,
dipping their sculpted wings,
watching me, keeping cold eyes
fixed on all I thought was mine.

East Running Spring

I.

Some looked into the water and saw nothing,
or more rightly said, looked through the water
into the mirror at the flame of the candle,
and still saw nothing they would admit.
My mother would never peek, she claims,
but own her mother did, who showed her,
and me, where to find the secret spring
among the several that burbled up
from the muck of what the first settlers
called Bear Waller and Caney Creek.
You had to know to dip beneath a slate rock
just under the road-bank, where the grass
parted for a stream of pebbles and silt,
for a cold clear jet running just the opposite
direction of the main creek it fed into.

II.

My grandmother gazed with all her brothers
and sisters. "What I see is a casket," the oldest
boy, Ruble, said, "but I can't tell who's in it."
He was dead in a month, nineteen years old.
Their sister Delta, what she saw was the face
of a stranger, and she was married within a year,
her new husband the picture image of the man
she described that night, candles burning
on the table like the new moon of March.
Another sister, Minnie, saw a blackbird circling,
and Clyde made out the curved handle of a cane.
Others claimed to see only a blur, or a swirl
like the wind, or the force that makes water flow.

Upper Chambers

The faces watching us aren't always the faces
we are watching, or that we know are with us,
as in the snapshot on my nephew's phone
of my sister sitting on the couch, in a house
built by our great-grandfather, holding two
orange and white cats curled gently asleep,
while above them all, in a corner where wall
meets ceiling, another face stares straight
into the camera, bearded and unsmiling,
stranger to us all, keeping solemn watch over
the part of our world that also belongs to him.

Headlights in the Rain

Rain covers the Southeast tonight,
makes me restless in the late hours,
wishing to be in home country
where plastic flowers are windblown
on the gravestones of my people.
I can picture headlights on the road
between here and there, and bends
in the highway where pavement
yields to the shape of ridge lines.
Headlights in the rain, passing through
Lowland and Raven Hill, crossing
William Bean Gap, and Little
Sycamore Creek— Lone Mountain
straight as a spindle in the west.
My father drove these roads on his
way to the terminal in White Pine,
his blue and orange Roadway truck
waiting with its trailer already loaded,
his logbook tucked in a travel bag
with a change of clothes and some
little white pills to keep his eyes open.
I want to feel an engine churn tonight,
steady as surging blood, alive.

II

Except in Memory

My father stands by the leaning tobacco barn
in the pasture field above our house,
shaking mineral salt out of a 50-pound bag
into a long iron trough as his herd of white-faced,
red-coated Herefords crowd around him.
I will not see that scene again, except in memory,
and wish I had a photograph of it, or better still,
video that shows him park his pick-up
at an angle, 30 feet from the barn and the cattle.
Then he lifts the bag out of the truck bed,
throws it over his shoulder to carry to the crib,
and cuts the braided string with a pocketknife.
The cows know the sound of his voice--- they come
when he calls, they bob their heads, they lick the salt.

Certain Backroads

On certain backroads, my father returned to his
old voice, clear but quiet, leaning forward
with a hand lifted to point toward the field
he plowed behind a horse for one dollar a day.

He could not remember the speckled mare's name,
nor the horse his older cousin, Bitt Rouse,
who paid his wage, drove alongside him,
but he recalled the sweat, and the damp flanks.

He found the pond Clint Stiner drove his new
'46 Chevy pick-up truck into one night,
weaving toward home through Lay Holler
after half a jar of Flossie Miller's corn whiskey.

When we got to the tilting house, moss-grown,
small as a toolshed, where Benny Presley lived,
my father's voice wavered, and I could picture
old man Presley, half-century dead, nod as we pass.

Gingham

After seventy years, my mother still remembers
the pink-checked gingham dress her mother
made with the pedal-pumped sewing machine.
She walked downtown with her sister and cousins,
up Gay Street and across to Market Square,
each wearing a dress with a different color
pattern, collar cut, and shape of hemline.
Her face lights when she tells how strangers smiled
at them, and how they skipped and pranced past
storefronts, their arms locked together like
twirlers around the Maypoles of ancient days.
After seventy years, her hands lift as she threads
her story once more, reaching up to take hold
of that day and bring it down from the empty air.

Rocks

My mother and I planted the garden
by ourselves one year, after my father
plowed a spot, then left on a long haul
out of the South, across the Midwest,
into still coat-weather North Dakota.
We dug rocks with a hoe and a rake,
scooped mounds of soil for bean-hills
only to find more rocks underneath.
Nothing we planted would harvest
so fully as the slate and sandstone
we dumped into the roadside ditch.
Morning passed, and the sun held
its round thumb down on our backs.
We sweated through shirts,
and our fingertips blistered even
through brown jersey gloves.
Pepper plants love the full light,
while tomatoes will wither under
walnut trees—all roots need a cup
of water the first and second days
they are in the ground, but our rocks
flourished with no attention at all.

Dream of the Road that Leads My Mother Back to a Little Brown House in the Valley of Her Birth

"Technicolor," she said, like a scene from a movie
framed in front of her, but real enough
to walk through and touch the greenest leaves
she ever saw overhanging the fencerow.

The red hound her sister loved, Bess, should have run
forward to meet her, and some cousins, maybe
Anna Lou and Fred, or Hildra and Greg,
ought to have been playing jack-rocks in the yard,

and some commotion her daddy surely would
have stirred, wondering where she had been,
why she had missed dinner, but nobody played
her favorite games and nobody called for her.

How deep and rich the dirt that caked on her shoes.
She walked and walked but could not reach
the tall grass of the yard that led to her porch,
her mother, and the door she longed to open.

The Call of Strange Birds

I grew up on the edge of the forest,
awaiting my signal from the spirits,
wondering often of the old wars,
of how many people across time

had taken other lives on purpose,
because they felt sanctioned to it.
Soon, the leaves fallen on the ground
weren't enough to imagine them all,

the killers and the dead, the weapons
and the bodies. I feared their voices,
the call of strange birds, and the black
panther's cry like a human scream.

Old wars fought on this same ground,
blood drained there by chipped arrows,
hatchets, bullets misshapen by bone,
leaves dropping, deep red, all around.

The Log Chain

The omen does not always reveal its message,
and the oracle may not speak the language
of the living, or show the way to change
fate unwanted, keeping steadily out of sight,
waiting in the wings of the future.

My great-grandparents did not know
their son was going to die that summer,
nineteen years old, playing fiddle tunes
at a barn dance just across the ridge,
dropping to the floor like a chopped tree.

What they did know was that one evening,
in the peaceful hour past dinner and washing,
all the animals fed, and the children sent
afield to play, a red-hot log chain came rolling
out of the woods, like lightning made metal.

The chain cast sparks and gathered speed,
clipped saplings, shot over the dirt road
across their sheared bottomland, and vanished,
leaving them trembling and mute, a vision each
discerned as a sign after they buried their boy.

Tending

We handled every leaf of every plant,
from seed to market, replanting, suckering,
grading, all to see the sunlit sheen in the fields,
the low green glow of quick-ripening leaves,
promising the poundage of cash in hand.
Now that ground is used for grazing cattle,
or some years rows of melons and corn,
thriving under the blue shimmer of a sky
that once nourished our hand-crafted crops,
like dreams from childhood that seemed
so real they rest like trusted memories now.

Lens

The hawk tethered in the lens,
pinned to his branch by the picture
my daughter took of him.
Zoomed into focus from a hundred yards,
he looked easeful, at rest,
unaware that some other two-legged
creature might prey upon him.
At such distance, he never knew
he was caught, his feathers
not even ruffled by the shot.

Chipping Arrowheads

The man in fringed buckskins draws
the shape of an arrowhead on a sliver
of pink and cream Oklahoma flint,
then shows my daughter how to
chip away the stone's edges
with a sanded deer antler.
She presses the rock and the shape
appears. Vision coming into form,
notched at the base so she can tie it
with deer sinew to a cane-shaft.
In the half-hour this girl spends
tapping and flaking, threading
and tying, the man's pale blue eyes
drift into small sockets of sky.
My daughter's hands turn over
one another in ancient patterns,
fletching turkey feathers
so this arrow might take flight,
glide its way into chosen flesh.

Fawn in Sapsucker Woods

Happy to be sitting on the cool pond bank
in summer, stirring algae with long sticks,
my daughter and I watched tadpoles dart
around each other in wriggling circles.
She drew a quick breath and her eyes
popped wide when the first raindrops hit
the backs of our necks. All the old trees
around us shivered and turned their leaves.
"Uh-oh," she said, and we ran along the trail
back toward home, our little white house
with garter snakes in the baseboards,
until she drew up mid-step, held in place
by a pair of eyes nearly level to her own,
the fawn as frozen in surprise as the girl.
Even the raindrops appeared to pause in air
as we all came to realize the encounter,
until the doe voiced her hoarse scold,
"Back, back," she seemed to say.
They were gone with the white-flag-waving
flash of their tails, and the only sound
behind them was the rain resuming
its loud passage through leaf-heavy branches.

Pilot

Leaves scuttle by the deer trail, and my eyes
flash toward the sound, muscles clenched
as I squint to see the same uncoiling retreat
my father and I once spotted between

slate rocks beside our clean-running creek.
When he chopped it with a hoe-blade
more than a dozen babies, short as waterdogs,
spilled out and scattered into the briars.

My father called it the pilot snake,
and I imagined the quick unseen strike
of the Messerschmitt over London,
streaking red sun of the Kamikaze in descent.

But I heard also an echo of Pontius Pilate,
felt the betrayal of a serpent disguised
while in plain view, holding the power
to decide death, or commutation. I thought

of how many times I must have been spared,
gathering kindling from the woodpile, seining
minnows in the creek, digging for ancestral
treasures through the attic of the dairy shed.

Blunt copper arrow of its head, banded length
of muscle, frozen except the quivering tail,
having kept the stinging, swelling judgment
held tight within its hinged jaws.

Nothing Familiar

The world held us like a cup,
or a deep bowl the stew of our lives
could be poured into.
We lived in a valley, in foothills
of ancient mountains. The trees
waited for each generation to be born,
to keep them company as they watched
over us from high above.
I heard stories about grandmothers,
grandfathers, great, great-great, and beyond—
further back than we had pictures
or letters, or deeds with illegible names.
Each step I took across the upper ridges
landed deep inside a broad old footprint.
What to call it, a link in a chain,
leaf on a tree, step on an ascending ladder?
Nothing familiar contains it—more like dirt
pressing together in a shared piece of ground,
swelling with rain water, feeding roots
and the busy mouths of insects,
giving life to what it can never watch grow.

Honeycutt Grocery

In old times, there was a blind man at the till.
He counted the money by feel, with a child
always beside him to make certain no swindler
handed him a single and claimed it was a five.
Goods bought there were simple, preserved,
tin-packed, except the peaches and apples,
picked by younger hands from Honeycutt's
own orchard and weighed against a stone.
What went with his eyes, his customers surely
wondered, but the old man told no stories,
preferring hymns on the gospel radio for company,
letting salvation offer its deal on his own terms.

Siren

City music, serenade of flashing light,
fast-turning wheel, everyday action,
familiar as other sharp edges, ringing
like a blue jay's squeal on repeat-play.
I heard it so seldom in childhood
that I cannot unlearn the tightening
muscles, pulling myself in toward
the core, the still point from which
I can cup hand to ear, determine
where the terrible thing takes place.
If I heard the blare, the pain
was personal, happening to someone
I knew, a neighbor whose heart seized,
or uncle whose thigh was torn
from the bone by a slipping sawblade.
We lived so far out that only a slow
emergency waited for help, siren song
more often eulogy than cavalry call.

Particle

Two years ago, we were numb, like our muscles
had been lain upon by a person exactly
our own size and shape.

Two years ago, our nerves jangled like the filament
of a blown lightbulb.

Two years ago, we buried my father,
and still the grass over his grave
sprouts around a bald patch.

Two years ago, we waited for the stone to arrive.

The room where he died still seems to hold
some fine last particle of his breath.

After the Reunion

I am the only child in the picture,
my brother and sister both already
too old to have to stand for one.
My shirt is off because I had been running
after the geese with my cousin David.
Just a few years later, I would have been
embarrassed about that, but at seven
bare skin is just another part of nature.
My mother and grandmother stand
behind me, in short sleeves on a hot
Memorial Day. So many of my mother's
aunts and uncles line up beside us,
Azalee and Gene, Ruby and Edsel,
Minnie and Horn, June without Owen,
Joe and Ruby Jean, but Cotton
would not come out of the house
for the picture, and Mutt and Vivian
must not have made the trip from Pulaski,
where they ran the bus station and taxi cabs,
and Delta must have been having trouble
with Richard again and stayed home.
Few are still alive, though in the fading image
they appear like eternals, so vivid in the heat
and glare of the sun that they can never falter.
As soon as the shutters all clicked, I tore out
after the geese again, and now hardly recall another
moment from that day, as other cousins stepped
into my place to have their pictures taken among
the generations, more part of the past already
than the future, which I must meet without them.

The Hollow Trunk

The mailman saw the blacksnake first,
and said, "Dad gum, that's a big 'un,"
as he walked wide of his original path.
My sister and I had stepped to the porch
for a break from the long, slow,
impossible-to-accept death of our father
inside the house he lived in fifty years.
It was mid-morning, mid-June, late-life.
Kim Cox has carried the mail since
he took over from Jack Wright,
who finally retired his blue Jeep,
which was sometimes the only vehicle
that passed our house on summer days.
I recall that Kim is our third or fourth
cousin on my mother's side, through
his wife Linda, who was a Johnson.
One day he delivers the mail for my father
who is alive, and another, he brings it
for my father who is no longer alive.
The heat in June digs in early each day,
and my sister and I watch as the snake
holds his course through the grass
and stretches his white chin onto the hollow
old trunk of the catalpa tree.
He hardly appears to move as he climbs,
slow and rhythmic, straight up until
the full six feet of him reaches from
the ground to a perch where the tree splits.
I look down at the mail Kim has just
handed me, and when I look back up,
the snake has disappeared into the tree
as quickly as the hawk moth takes flight.

Elegy for an Afternoon

I know that my brother and I stood
beside the rail tracks in an empty lot,
him telling stories of our grandfather,
yet memory fails to ignite the image
I want from that day, which is to see
his face working as he circled his way
through how the old man played tricks
on our grandmother, her stern face
breaking into laughter as I never saw.
I know that we had plates of spaghetti
for lunch at Louie's Italian Restaurant,
and JFG Coffee at the short-lived café
beside their downtown roasting house.
Overhead, the paraffin sweep of sky,
clouds melted by the sun they tried
to conceal, ground birds scrap-hunting
all around us, the day getting so quickly
away, faster even than my brother's face,
which I have not seen for ten long years,
and will not see in any years ahead.

Paper Treasures

We traded baseball cards or comic books,
and sold them for cash, my brother and I.
Flea markets and antique shops,
thrift stores, wherever junk came to rest,
we excavated paper treasures.
I watched how he measured the edges
for crispness, or the smudge of fingerprints--
it made me a shrewd observer,
connoisseur of the thrown-away.
He set valuables free more easily than I did,
always the collector, holding on to things.
Even now, see how effortlessly he let go
the whole world, and how I cling
to a memory of riches we did not even save.

Self-Portrait

Water currents dig deeper into the earth
over time, as living digs deeper into flesh.
Faces carry the imprint of all the hands
that have brushed across their surfaces;

all the smiles and frowns and vague
glances make contact with the skin.
I can see their impressions along
my cheekbones, down my jaw line,

seeking shelter under gray stubble.
Something behind the eyes like rain
waiting to fall, that the second round
of changes has just begun, the loosening,

the body letting go of itself.
There is a future in our faces,
history with secrets not yet revealed,
with only one certainty hidden from view.

I wish I had never stepped around the curtain
to see my brother on that hospital gurney,
wish I had never seen the death-mask of Keats,
never looked at the mirror in this dark room.

Beneath the Birch Trees

Nearing eighty, my mother's attention
is drawn to focus by the several kinds
of moss that grow in the woods above
the pond my father dug when I was boy.

"Have there always been so many colors
of green?" she wonders aloud as we collect
handful after handful of various shades,
as furry and moist as an otter's coat.

Neither of us knows the names of these
distinct species, or the varieties of ferns
that uncurl beneath the birch trees
and thrive in shadow of the cedars.

She asks me what kind of hawk watches
her chickens from the lowest branch
of the pear tree, and which sparrow
wears the yellow streak across its cheek.

Voice

Here my parents strolled
around the family cemetery,
my mother's people buried
in land my father tended.
I come alone to join them
this late September evening—
first cool winds of the season
blowing heavy clouds between
me and the crisp blue beyond.

Gravestones bear the names
of our personal history,
so many who came and went
before my time began.
In the soft voice of a mind
addressing itself, the interior
sound only I can ever hear:
"Someday you will come here
and never leave."

Sojourner

I cannot say why they picked this place,
why they stopped moving where they did,
those ancestors of mine who settled
in this steep tangle of over- and undergrowth.

They started from outskirts of glorious cities
of the eighteenth century— Heidelberg, Rotterdam,
Philadelphia— before some wayward gene
rejected that life, some code imprinted

in the blood line that led me back
from my own private Ithaca,
where the valleys and lakes stretch
invisible wings around a sojourner.

I cannot get close enough to the forever-
sunken spot, homeland beneath the lake,
where they built log cabins and plank barns,
turned stony soil for scattering their seeds.

Cut loose from the vision they must have had,
I strain my eyes to see, to dig my fingers
deep into the dirt, to turn my mind toward
that long-ago time, to dream it as my own.

The Moon and the North Star

I walk out late to listen for the owl.
Some nights I hear him from the bedroom,
while other evenings he keeps quiet, or patrols
another corner of the neighborhood
for moles, rats, or late-feeding starlings.
The moon, the North Star, grass grown
thick from a week's rain and sun, and a few
streets back, in a leafier section of town,
a car horn taps twice, and the owl answers,
two quick calls, pressing his eternal question.

A Blue Tractor Passing

It was a New Holland or an older model Ford
that we could hear coming for half a mile
before it reached the house. When I asked my mother
if she recognized the driver, a stranger to me,
she said, "I wish it was K.O. Campbell and that
your daddy was standing down there
beside the road to throw his hand up at him."
K.O. drove my school bus, in addition to the one
blue tractor on Cain Road, and some years for
Christmas he brought us a bottle of his homemade
wine— apple, pear, elderberry— which were
the only spirits we ever kept in the house.
K.O. outlived my father by just about a year,
and now the Beasons tend his orphaned herd.
His bull still jumps the fence sometimes, and my
nephews cross him back over while our cows bawl—
like my mother and me, these cattle keep looking
for the old farmers who softly spoke their true names
as they scattered salt into empty feed troughs.

Acknowledgments

The author gratefully acknowledges the following publications where poems in this collection first appeared, sometimes in slightly different form:

Appalachian Heritage ("Barn Swallows"); Blackbird ("Katie Myers"); The Goliad Review ("Distant Star" and "Lens"); Louisiana Literature ("Chipping Arrowheads" and "Holocene"); Now & Then Magazine ("Hawks"); The Pikeville Review ("East Running Spring" and "Upper Chambers"); Prairie Schooner ("Except in Memory" and "Old Man Wandering the Roads"); Sacred Trespasses ("Mossy Springs"); Still: The Journal ("Jewel," "Raft," and "Siren"); Valparaiso Poetry Review ("Elegy for an Afternoon" as "Elegy")

"History" and "Nothing Familiar" first appeared in Appalachian Reckoning: A Region Responds to Hillbilly Elegy, West Virginia University Press, 2019

"The Kingdom of the Dead" first appeared in Missouri Review Online "Poem of the Week" feature, 2012

"October Woods" and "Voice" first appeared in Mountains Piled upon Mountains: Appalachian Nature Writing from the Anthropocene, West Virginia University Press, 2019

"Pilot" first appeared in A Field Guide to Southern Appalachia, University of Georgia Press, 2019

"Wind Work" first appeared in Anthology of Appalachian Writers, Volume IX, Shepherd University Press, 2017

With thanks to the many friends who helped these poems come to their own way of being.